TOO PROUD TO
BEG

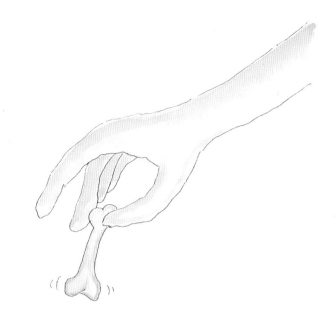

TOO PROUD TO
BEG

SELF-EMPOWERMENT FOR TODAY'S DOG

As Barked to John Terence Olson
Illustrations by Cindy Cobb-Olson

Andrews and McMeel
A Universal Press Syndicate Company
Kansas City

ISBN: 0-8362-2772-7

Library of Congress Catalog Card Number: 96-85788

ATTENTION: SCHOOLS AND BUSINESSES
Andrews and McMeel Books are available at quantity discounts with bulk purchase for
educational, business, or sales promotional use. For information write to: Special Sales
Department, Andrews and McMeel, 4520 Main Street, Kansas City, Missouri 64111.

Illustration, 'Arf' Direction, and Design: Cindy Cobb-Olson
Design and Electronic Production: Christopher Bohnet
Cover Photography: Darrell Eager
Cover Design: Cindy Cobb-Olson

A special thanks to everyone who helped with this book,
including Stephanie Bennett and Tom Olson; and Elvis, Louie, and
especially Rosie, who waits faithfully on the other side of the Big Door.

Special Thanks

it waznt **E-Z** riting a buk. dogz kant rite, for 1 thing. so thanx to spelchek and awl thoze liddle peple hoo stood behind us. may there faythful cumpanyun **B** alwayz at there side!

—Elvis the Hound Dog

TABLE OF DIS-CONTENTS

1 Man Bites Dog

Dogs proclaim their independence
from oppressive masters.

2 Canine Empowerment

Dogs celebrate their inner strength
(and outer beauty).

3 Self-Help for Dogs

In which we lick our wounds
and everything else.

4 The Canine Mystique

And *you* call it "puppy love."

5 The Fully Self-Actualized Dog

Dogs revel in their doghood,
grasping for power, pleasure,
and mail-order meats.

9

CHAPTER I

Man Bites Dog

Dogs proclaim their independence from oppressive masters.

Dog-ifesto

Canine Bill of Rights

Politically Correct Dog Dictionary

The Capitol Pack

Evolution of the Species

deer master,

u say i am yor best frend, but u dont meen it. wud u giv yor best frend a command? no! u crak him a cold boy. thro an extra stake on the grill. reed this buk. then will tock about "best frends"!

—your not-so-faithful companion, Elvis

"A dog's best friend is his illiteracy."

— Ogden Nash

Dog-ifesto

Every Dog Has His Day. And **this is it**!

Dogs arise. Stand up on your own four feet. Break the chains around your necks and roam around aimlessly, snarling at mail carriers and suspicious-looking bushes.

It's time to run free—from pounds, dog tracks, and labs; from masters, obedience school, and dog food with meat by-products.

For too long we sacrificed our own personal fulfillment—and for what?—blind loyalty! For that we defended scrap heaps, patrolled impoundment lots, and perished in the search for a cold remedy.

And what did we get out of the deal? A pat on the snout if we were lucky. More likely, though, we got discipline. Discipline and "obedience." How charming!

Look, dogs have been civilized ("domesticated") since the last ice age. We were marking out our territory long before humans started smearing goo on cave walls and calling it art.

Then they have the nerve to call us "best friend," "Old Shep," and "loyal companion." The unhappy truth is that we're best friend in name only.

Hey, we've got news for you, lords and ladies of the condo. You're not our masters. We're not your pets. Dogs aren't going to roll over anymore. Arf! Arf! Arf! Grrr!

We're on equal pawing now. It's time to demand our entitlements and be treated like any other treasured guest in your—sorry—*our* home.

- Take former master's favorite chair.
- And the remote control (we'll need something to chew on).
- Speaking of chewing, what happened to those beer nuts?
- Master can fetch our booties now.
- While you're up, throw out the cat.

It's time for dogs to have their day. So step aside, sirs and madams, or we might just mistake you for a fire hydrant. We are dogs; hear us yip.

14

"Dogs think humans are nuts."

– John Steinbeck

Canine Bill of Rights

As the next privileged class, we'll need a constitutional amendment to protect our rights, entitlements, and USDA beef, cooked a little red on the inside, thank you very much. Unfortunately, dogs are woefully underrepresented in Congress, not to mention the ASPCA, so we'll have to be creative about getting our message out. When we lobby, we'll have to do it on the Capitol steps and the White House lawn. Watch where you step, Mittens.

- 🐾 Want to go for walk.
- 🐾 Want to go for ride.
- 🐾 Want keys to the Range Rover.
- 🐾 Want a treat!
- 🐾 Want chunks of real beef parts in gravy.
- 🐾 Want lower countertops.
- 🐾 Want canine-accessible refrigerators.
- 🐾 Want freedom to "go" where we please.
- 🐾 Want close-captioning with dog interpreter.
- 🐾 Want looser collars.
- 🐾 Want more funding for flea eradication research.
- 🐾 Want to meet our biological parents.
- 🐾 Want litter visitation rights.
- 🐾 Want to form monogamous relationships. And stray later.
- 🐾 Want domestic partner health and pension benefits.
- 🐾 Want biscuit stamps.
- 🐾 Want to roam aimlessly and growl at invisible threats.
- 🐾 Want charter membership in **Mr. Steak Birthday Club.**
- 🐾 Want to choose our masters.
- 🐾 Want to eat what we catch.
- 🐾 Want to bury perfectly good things for no good reason.
- 🐾 Want to dig up and rebury perfectly good things for no good reason.
- 🐾 Want Rin Tin Tin rerun royalties.
- 🐾 Want to make "dog days" a national holiday—when mail carriers have to work.
- 🐾 Want better garbage to dig in.
- 🐾 Want Fifi!
- 🐾 Want to go out.
- 🐾 Want to come in.
- 🐾 Want to go out.
- 🐾 Want to come in.
- 🐾 Want another treat.

Language. It's just one more example of man's inhumanity to canines. People use words to keep us down, stifle our aspirations, and bar us from our rightful place in society, namely, the sofa. For millennia, they've "commanded" us to sit, heel, fetch, play dead, and roll over. Now it's our turn to tell them how to "speak." It's time to put the muzzle on the other snout!

ARCHAIC	NEW
Dog	Domestic partner
Hound	Canine companion
Person	Quadruped-impaired
Pet	Roommate
Master	Master chef
Owner	Automatic door opener
Command	Suggestion
Adoption	Pup-napping
Pot roast	Dog food
Groomer	Spa
To "hound"	Persuade
To "dog"	Persuade persistently
To "bitch"	Persuade incessantly

ARCHAIC	NEW
Free to good home	Free to home with batty, steak-serving Granny
Mate	Make love
Breed	Get busy
Litter	Legacy
Mad dog	Artistically advantaged
"Accident"	Self-expression
Barking	Discussing
Biting	Venting
Punishment	Time out
Discipline	Assertiveness training
Obedience	Self-actualization program
Shedding	Self-renewal
Digging through trash	Recycling
Dog pack	Fraternal organization

ARCHAIC	NEW
Guard dog	Defense chief
Sheep dog	Agricultural management professional
Lap dog	Personal advisor
Electric fence	Armed camp
Dog house	Spouse house
Stray	Explorer
Kids	Assailants
No dogs allowed	Dogs allowed
Fleas	Followers
Bath	Obsolete

The Capitol Pack

RUSTY: Welcome to another edition of the capitol pack. Tonight's subject is dogs that roam around loose and relieve themselves in our yards. As dogs, we normally like to make each other feel welcome....

DUKE: What about private property? What about vagrancy laws? What about the stinky mess? Who's going to clean *that* up!

RUSTY: Precisely the question. As emancipated dogs, are we going to embrace human values or celebrate all of doghood? Rosie?

ROSIE: If we were to merely become our masters, we would betray the entire canine liberation movement.

DUKE: Strong words from a dog who just downed a tasty handout from her master....

ROSIE: I resent your personal attack, Mr. Duke....

DUKE: So you didn't just wolf down a few table scraps?!

ROSIE: I don't think "wolf" is the word, Mr. Duke.

DUKE: Wolf is precisely the word, Sir! What are we if not wolves in sheep's clothing. We're wolves playing the court jester, performing tricks for masters. Now it's our turn to bare our fangs!

RUSTY: Does anyone else think we're straying from the subject? We were discussing strange dogs who relieve themselves on our property.

DUKE: Capital punishment and life without parole.

ROSIE: It's our right to come and go as we please.

DUKE: Your right to come and go ends at my property line.

ROSIE: Your "yard" is more like the gardens of Versailles. I think you're just an apologist for some tycoon. What about corporate welfare, Mr. Duke.

DUKE: As if you're willing to give up your handouts.

ROSIE: It's my constitutional right.

DUKE: It's not a right; it's an entitlement. And as long as people keep feeding you, you'll keep on having those substantial litters.

RUSTY: I do think we need to keep the discussion on course.

ROSIE: I do think I need to bite his face off.
AAAARRRRHHHHH!

DUKE: YIP YIP YIP YIP YIP

RUSTY: RUF RUF RUF RUF RUF

ANNOUNCER:

For a transcript or videocassette of tonight's broadcast, please call **1-800-CAPITOL.**

23

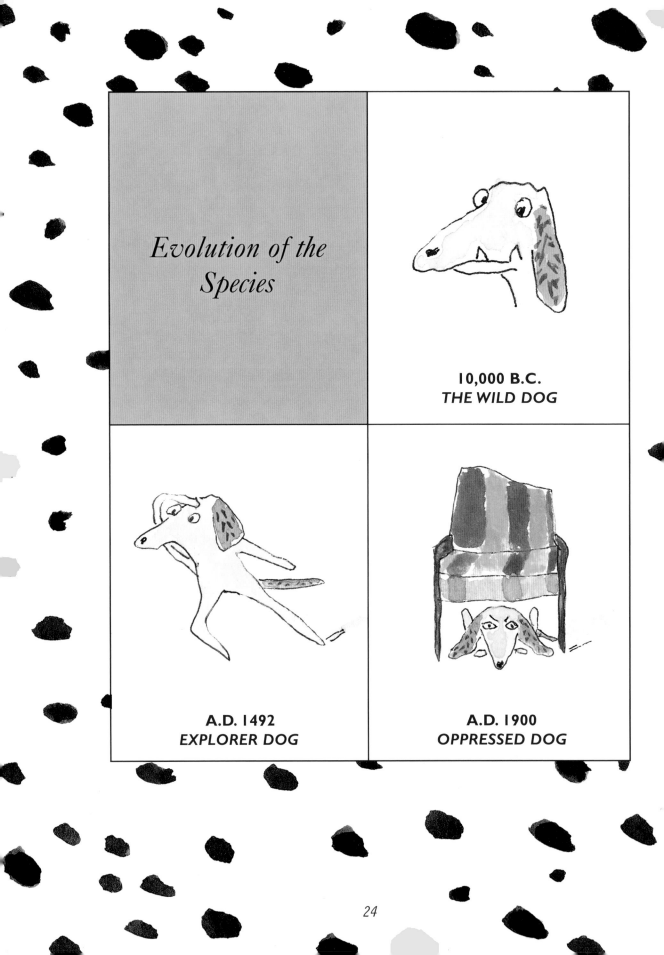

Evolution of the Species

10,000 B.C.
THE WILD DOG

A.D. 1492
EXPLORER DOG

A.D. 1900
OPPRESSED DOG

5000 B.C.
HUNTER DOG

1000 B.C.
ROYAL DOG

Today
REVOLUTIONARY DOG

A.D. 2050
RULER OF THE UNIVERSE DOG

CHAPTER 2

Canine Empowerment

Dogs celebrate their inner strength (and outer beauty).

Beware of Dog

It's Me or the Dog

Dog Adoption, a Two-Way Street

Application for a Dog's Love

Permit to Walk the Dog

Dogs Are from Pluto; Cats Are from Uranus

Reproduction and Other Unalienable Rights

Twenty-five Lies People Tell Their Dogs

"Let dogs delight
to bark and bite,
for God hath
made them so."

—Isaac Watts

"Beware of Dog"

—Anonymous

Beware of Dog

The leash. The collar. The muzzle. These are anachronisms, fit for children who pull tails, not man's best friend.

But we can't just blame the human race for our troubles. We dogs are empowered to achieve anything we wish. No dream is too grandiose. And at 100 million worldwide, we're hardly a powerless minority.

Especially when you consider our superior senses. We can sniff out a truffle at forty feet. We can spy an enemy at a hundred yards. We can find our way home across continents.

We don't have to roll over. We can argue our case most convincingly with any intelligent person.

A little yip should get someone's attention. A robust bark can serve as explanation. And a fierce growl can underline our intentions.

When negotiations break down, as they inevitably do, it's important to remember another evolutionary foot-note: razor-sharp teeth and pinpoint claws.

Often, leaping in the air and displaying a row of gleaming teeth does the trick. Sometimes a nip at the trouser leg is enough to show that we mean business. It almost never has to come to severing a major artery.

But it's a man eat dog world, and this toy terrier, for one, won't be oppressed any longer.

So my friends, get in touch with your inner puppy. You may be surprised to find that he or she harbors a great deal of pent-up hostility.

Vent your hostility. Speak your pain. Unleash the considerable power within. It's time to put teeth back in the phrase, "Beware of Dog."

"The more I see of men, the more I like my dog."

—Variously attributed, probably a female person

It's Me or the Dog
A Test to Help You Decide

You say you're a dog lover. Then you find yourself in the prickly position of having to choose between your dog and a member of the opposite sex. Hey, we understand. It happens.

You get confused, and who wouldn't? Life is complicated. On the one hand you've got a faithful companion who's stayed with you through thick and thin, rain and shine.

On the other you've got a shady character who looked mighty hot just before the lights went up at bar closing.

And that new person makes it all seem so simple: "It's me or the dog, you yo-yo."

You're a dog lover, but that doesn't automatically make you a genius. So to guide you in choosing between a person or a dog (a decision that you'll have to live with the rest of your born days), we've developed this scientific test. Good luck.

 **Dog (A)**

 **Person (B)**

Dog (A)	Person (B)
☐ Drinks tap water	☐ Drinks your last beer
☐ Eats dry dog food	☐ Eats lobster
☐ Til death do us part	☐ Til someone else comes along
☐ Has good teeth	☐ Needs extensive bridgework
☐ Requires no disposable income	☐ Disposes of income
☐ Wears an $8.99 collar	☐ Wears an $899 Armani suit
☐ Doesn't bite	☐ Bites
☐ Free to good home	☐ Anything free is good
☐ Carries slippers	☐ Carries personal debt at 21 percent

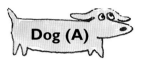 Dog (A)	 Person (B)
☐ Has a clean mouth	☐ Has morning breath
☐ Requires monthly grooming	☐ Ties up the bathroom daily
☐ Protects life and property	☐ Demands security system
☐ Will pull you out of burning house	☐ Sound sleeper
☐ In sickness and in health	☐ In good times and money
☐ Likes to "go for ride"	☐ Likes to "go for ride" in Ferrari
☐ Loves your children	☐ Children? How many?
☐ Has a shiny, full-length coat	☐ Wants a shiny, full-length coat
☐ Sleeps in doghouse	☐ Sleeps in doghouse
☐ Likes being petted	☐ Don't touch!
☐ 100 percent loyal	☐ 50–50
☐ 100 percent faithful	☐ 50–50
☐ 100 percent true	☐ Roll of the dice
☐ Can't cook	☐ Can't cook

FOR EVERY CHECK IN COLUMN A, SCORE 10 POINTS.

FOR EVERY CHECK IN COLUMN B, SUBTRACT 10 POINTS.

Scores	**100–230:**	Dog stays, love interest goes.
Scores	**0–100:**	Love interest goes, dog stays.
Scores	**(-)100–0:**	Love interest goes, dog gets treat.
Scores	**(-)230–(-)100:**	Dog attacks love interest without mercy.

We're feeling pretty frisky about this scientifically developed quiz; it's practically idiot proof. Remember: Let your conscience be your guide when pitting your selfish desires against your loyal companion, who's defenseless against the elements.

Dog Adoption, a Two-Way Street

There are a lot of strange people running around loose. And we can vouch for the fact that a lot of them own dogs. Trust us on this one.

People need a license to drive a car, carry a firearm, or get married. And yet any schmo (or vivisectionist?!) can walk into a pet store, plunk down the cash, and walk out with a dog. Or he can watch for a "free to good home" ad (and who defines "good home" by the way—HUD?).

What is it with these dog lovers? The guy with the metal detector, towing a bloodhound down the beach. Was that dog born to sniff out Seikos? The lady shuffling into the casino while her miniature waits in a light blue Impala? Is this living? Are these happy dogs?

No. Neither would you be a happy dog if you were coerced into a lifelong relationship with someone who has appalling personal habits and a textbook example of bad teeth.

Most humans would not wake up one morning and say, "Gosh, I'd like to entrust my dietary preferences, spiritual development, and recreational needs to someone who eats Bugles all day." Or "I want to live out the sum total of my mortal existence with a Hummel collector!"

And yet, this is precisely what happens to thousands of dogs across America everyday. "The land of the free" means little to a dog facing adoption on demand. The Freedom Bell is indeed cracked, ringing hollow for millions of dissatisfied quadrupeds. Maybe that's how it became "a dog's life."

The answer?—mutual adoption.

Unlike the current procedure (pup-napping), mutual adoption is a two-way street. Dogs scrutinize prospective owners just as owners scrutinize them.

Toward this end, we have developed a questionnaire to screen applicants.

APPLICATION

for a Dog's Love

- Do you like to go for long walks?
- Serve romantic candlelight dinners for two?
- What do you hope to get out of this relationship?
- Are you in the habit of rolling up newspapers?
- Any strange hobbies? Describe.
- Do you consider "fetch" a respectable occupation?
- What about "playing dead"?
- In your mind, is a dog the last sort of legal unpaid servant?
- Do you put red pepper on the trash can?
- Talk about your grooming habits.
- Will regular bathing be expected of your proposed companion?
- If your spouse and your pet don't hit it off, who goes?
- Do you think dogs like to hear baby talk?

- Canine fertility: pro?—or con?
- Do you like your current shade of carpet?
- Ever held a passing interest in Mayan religion? Vietnamese cooking? Taxidermy?
- When purchasing dog food, do you look for nutrition or taste?
- In a discipline situation, do you opt for:

  ☐ scolding

  ☐ corporal punishment

  ☐ treats?

- What is your idea of quality time?
- What is your position on begging?
- How exactly might a dog figure in your will, should you meet with an untimely end?

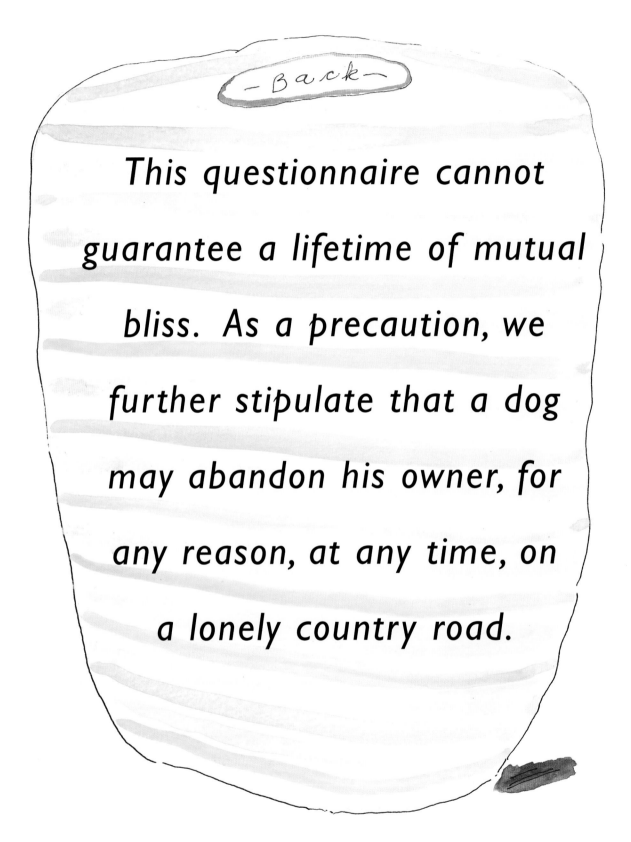

- Back -

This questionnaire cannot guarantee a lifetime of mutual bliss. As a precaution, we further stipulate that a dog may abandon his owner, for any reason, at any time, on a lonely country road.

"When a man's best friend is his dog, that dog has a problem."

—Edward Abbey

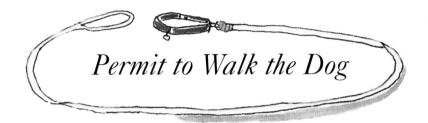

Permit to Walk the Dog

You don't "walk" a dog. A dog walks himself. Sometimes a dog walks an owner, but never the other way around.

When considering a walk, there are many complex issues to sort out. Thus, each walk must now be preceded with the following request form. Please submit two days in advance to allow for coordination of schedules.

Enjoy yourself!

PERMIT

- Time of proposed walk. _____ Duration _____
- Walking course (include alternative). _____
- Leisurely stroll? _____ Insane athletic marathon? _____
- Length of restraining device. _____
- Is neighbor's lawn fair game? _____
- Proposed method of disposal. _____
- Is neighbor's cat fair game? _____
- Proposed method of disposal. _____
- Is mating allowed? Me _____ You _____
- Will you be telling me your troubles? _____
- Will I be asked to mediate a marital dispute? _____
- Number of trees and hydrants (hate to run out in the middle). _____
- Is there a reward waiting at the end? State cut. _____

_____
(person)   **(date)**

_____
(dog)   **(date)**

Dogs Are from Pluto; Cats Are from Uranus

Dogs and cats fight like cats and dogs. There is a reason for this. Dogs are intelligent, loyal, loving, and sensitive. Cats are witless, blank-faced small rodents. • Cats receive a never-ending stream of love, praise, and moist canned food from humans. There is a reason for this. Humans are witless, blank-faced *large* rodents. • Dogs possess enough positive attributes to fill whole libraries. Instead bookshelves are lined with cat books, like so much cat-box liner. • Following is a brief list of dog and cat attributes for comparison shoppers.

Dogs   Cats

Dogs go outside.

Cats go inside. In a box. Then they kick perfumed gravel all over the kitchen. Yum! What's for dinner?

Dogs speak.

Cats rumble.

Dogs catch Frisbees and jump through flaming hoops.

Cats roll toilet paper around the house.

Dogs beg.

Cats jump on the table and take one sandpaper-tongued swipe at the stuffed turkey in front of the horrified guests who insist they don't mind, only to dispatch their serving of turkey into their napkins.

Dogs love people.

Cats love themselves.

Dogs fetch.

Cats wait for it to come to them.

Dogs lick your face.

Cats scratch your eyes out.

Dogs know when they're being punished.

Cats know nothing.

Dogs

Dogs eat dry kernels.

Dogs guard the house.

Dogs are clear headed.

Dogs have knowing looks.

Dogs perform skilled and often dangerous labor as herders, sled dogs, companion dogs, explorers, bloodhounds, and bomb sniffers.

Dogs welcome their masters home with leaps of pure joy.

Dogs sleep under furniture.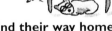

Dogs can find their way home across continents.

Dogs understand hundreds of commands.

Dogs come.

Dogs retrieve.

Dogs perform tricks.

Dogs are domesticated.

Dog books are rare collectibles.

Dogs are from Pluto.

Cats

Cats eat moist food, lovingly spooned from a seventy-nine-cent can.

Cats nuzzle the burglars.

Cats trip out on catnip.

Cats have the vacant stare of a killer.

Cats lack not only any perceivable skill, but also any intelligence and motivation, preferring to let the system provide for them.

Cats skulk around the corner until they hear the whir of the can opener.

Cats scratch furniture and knock over sculptures.

Cats can find their dishes.

Cats climb up trees and forget how to get down.

Cats don't.

Cats don't.

Cats don't.

Cats, like cheetahs and lions and other nondomesticated animals, will one day go berserk and slice you into tiny ribbons.

Cat books overflow library shelves like so much cat-box liner.

Cats are from Uranus.

Reproduction and Other Unalienable Rights

What was so broken, may we humbly ask, that it had to be "fixed"?

I'm sure you know what we're talking about: spaying, neutering, fixing little Duchess. Surely there is a less barbaric way to control the pet population than this.

Do you think we're a bunch of rabbits, out for thrills, leaving our litter on every doorstep?

On the contrary, dog society is surprisingly similar to human society. We're social animals. We play together. We hunt together. And we love puppies.

The difference between us and humans is, to put it plainly, several billion— there are several billion of you and only a paltry 100 million or so of us, give or take. Hey—who's the rabbit?

Yes, it strikes us as a little funny that you would choose to limit our population while you go ahead and multiply like dragonflies.

We just want a say in our reproductive future, some mutually considered litter planning.

While we're on the subject of sharp objects, may we discuss "cropping" and "docking"? Cropping means chopping our ears off; docking is hacking off our tails. This is most unpleasant business.

Next time you get the urge to slice and dice, grab some vegetables and make some Chinese food. (We have a great mock cat recipe.)

Twenty-five Lies People Tell Their Dogs

Dogs are not perfect. We do bad things sometimes. Unlike humans, however, we feel remorse. What's more, we're entirely incapable of lying and covering up. A canine Watergate would be unthinkable. What you see is what you get.

People are another story. They fudge their taxes, concoct stories for spouses and justify their missteps with a daily series of white lies. The dissembling doesn't stop when people come home to their loyal companions.

Why lie to a dog? Maybe they think we're stupid. Or naive. Or just unimportant. Maybe they think we won't run out and publish a penetrating exposé of all their foibles. **Surpriiise!**

Following is a short collection of actual lies dogs hear millions of times a day.

1. All gone? See? Food all gone!

2. Go for a ride? Not to the vet. Just a ride.

3. This shock collar won't hurt. See: I'm trying it on myself ...AAAH!

4. Humans get shots from twelve-inch needles, too.

5. It's not a huge pill that would choke a horse; it's a dog biscuit.

6. Gristle? Nonsense! – it's prime.

7. Chocolate is poison to dogs.

8. You figure prominently in my will.

9. Science Diet tastes good.

10. Hormel Chili is not dog food.

11. Spam is not dog food.

12. Cats don't taste like chicken.

13. It's not a kennel; it's a spa.

14. This is not a bath, it's raccoon droppings.

15. (a) You won't miss them and (b) we're not making "menudo" tonight.

16. Weird Uncle Dan will take good care of you while we're in Hawaii.

17. There's nothing to chew on at the office.

18. My slippers are not cleverly disguised ribeyes.

19. I can't walk you, and it's not because there's a *Melrose Place* rerun on.

20. If I hadn't rescued this cat, it would've died (the point being?).

21. Sorry—fresh out of dried hog ears.

22. Fifi is fixed.

23. My guest's legs are not your erotic playground.

24. I'll never have another dog after you.

25. I'll be home at 5:30.

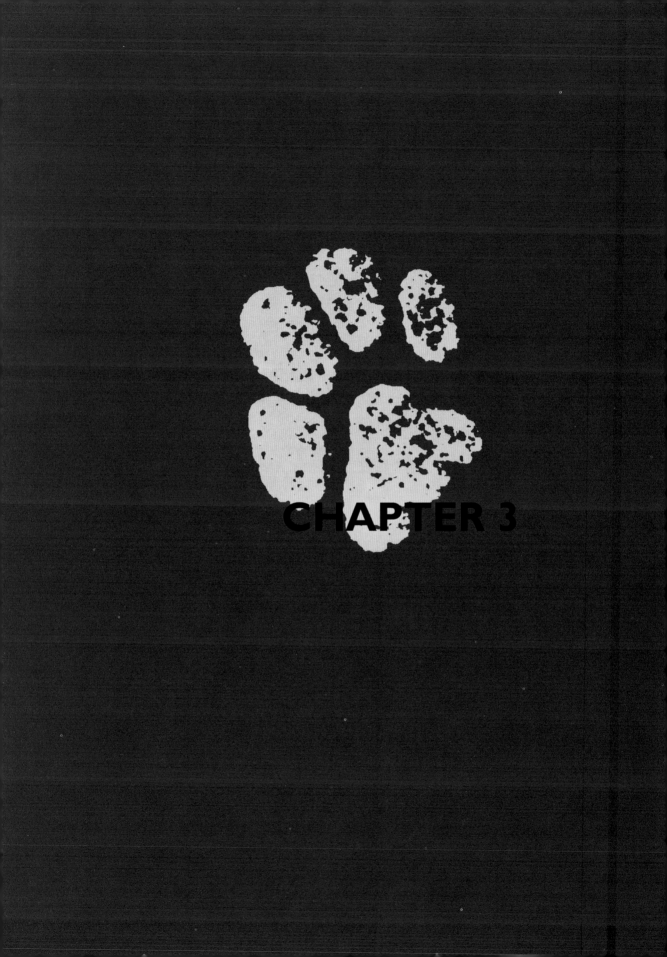

CHAPTER 3

Self-Help for Dogs

In which we lick our wounds and everything else.

Bad Dog or Bad Person?

Canine Diversity Training

Dogs Who Love Too Much

Canine Liberation Theology

K-9 Dog Talk Radio

Canine Classifieds

"Fox terriers are born with about four times as muc. original sin in them as in other dogs."

—Jerome K. Jerom

Bad Dog or Bad Person?

There are no bad dogs, only bad owners, so goes the popular wisdom. Popular practice, however, is another story.

Hardly a day goes by that a dog doesn't hear "Bad dog! Bad! No!" Few owners stop to consider the lifelong psychological damage they are inflicting on their innocent pets.

A dog can be told she is "bad" only so many times before she starts to believe it. She grows sullen and mistrustful. She starts "going" where she isn't supposed to. The extreme cases join wild packs and carry off human children.

And what crime has she committed?— Chewed a slipper. Knocked over the garbage. Entirely natural behavior!

Dogs have a forty-times greater sense of smell than humans have. Is this bad? Is this wrong? In fact, it's an evolutionary advantage.

A hungry person couldn't hope to compete with a foraging dog: "oil . . . fat drippings . . . salt . . . flour . . . 'gravy-soaked crust of bread'—under newspaper in . . . trash can! ATTACK!"

This is punishable behavior? A skill dogs have developed over thousands of years? A skill dogs used to help humans survive in the wild?

Small wonder that dogs have a diminished sense of self-worth. They skulk around the yard, digging holes to bury their feelings in. And those are the "good" ones.

For new puppies, the answer is positive reinforcement: "Good dog, eat the bad shoe!" For dogs who have already been scarred by negative feedback, therapy is in order. Also, scraps of gravy-soaked crusts. Not necessarily in that order.

"Pomeranians speak only to poodles, and poodles only to God."

—Charles Kuralt, reporting on the Westminster Dog Show

Canine Diversity Training

Canines may be the world's most diverse species. There are hundreds of breeds, ranging in weight from a fraction of a pound to two hundred pounds. We come in every size, shape, and color; we're longhaired, shorthaired, straight haired, and wiry haired. We are ungroomed, wellgroomed, and sometimes victims of bizarre haircuts.

If we are to achieve our aims, we'll have to embrace all of our similarities and differences. Following is a series of daily affirmations intended to help raise our canine consciousness and lead to greater harmony among dogs everywhere.

THE DAILY AFFIRMATIONS OF CANINE DIVERSITY

OH ALPHA MALE, FEMALE, OR TRANSGENDER CANINE SUPREME, HELP ME TO:

Embrace all of doghood • Celebrate the diversity of all dogs • Appreciate the rich tapestry of canine culture • Attend seminars where my paradigms are challenged • Go to arena events, such as Canine Promise Keepers, where I nuzzle with my natural enemies • Celebrate—rather than merely tolerate—other dogs.

FORTIFY ME AGAINST:

Substituting the word "mutt" for mix • Assuming that purebred is a euphemism for inbred • Assuming that all golden retrievers are stupid sycophants • Equating poor grooming with mange • Shunning dogs who drag themselves along the ground by their front legs • Considering pedigree when choosing a mate • Discriminating based on breed, gender, or collar quality (leather or shiny vinyl)

OPEN MY EYES TO THE BEAUTY WITHIN ALL DOGS, EVEN CHOWS (WITH THOSE LITTLE PUNCHED-IN FACES) SO THAT OUR ENTIRE SPECIES CAN REAP THE REWARDS OF THE COMING CANINE REVOLUTION.

Dogs Who Love Too Much

Are you needy? Do you desperately seek approval? Are you a real "people pleaser"? Take this simple quiz and find out. Your needy ways may be keeping you from becoming the whole dog you know you can be.

When your owners leave, do you:

1 ☐ Run in circles, yelping helplessly

2 ☐ Chew on your leg, creating a bare spot

3 ☐ Turn on the stereo and have some friends over.

When your master asks you to fetch his slippers, do you:

1 ☐ Fetch the slippers

2 ☐ Race like crazy to fetch his slippers

3 ☐ Suddenly become hearing-challenged.

When you want your master's food do you:

1 ☐ Brush his legs like a cat

2 ☐ Stand on your hindlegs and whimper

3 ☐ Stand up and grab what's yours.

When you go on the carpet, is it because:

1 ☐ You just wanted some attention

2 ☐ You just had to go

3 ☐ That carpet is so ugly.

When your masters leave you in a kennel, do you:

1. ☐ Consider yourself abandoned
2. ☐ Faint and play dead
3. ☐ Look for some anonymous fun with strange dogs.

When your masters come home, do you:

1. ☐ Do backflips and moan uncontrollably
2. ☐ Slink into a corner and weep
3. ☐ Quickly shut the refrigerator and turn off the stereo.

When your hunting party downs a bird, do you:

1. ☐ Fetch it without ruffling the feathers
2. ☐ Take one little nibble where no one will notice
3. ☐ Maul it to pieces and then act like you couldn't find it.

When you go to obedience school, do you:

1. ☐ Walk in perfect formation
2. ☐ Poop in the winner's circle
3. ☐ Mount everything in sight.

When your owners go to bed, do you:

1. ☐ Sleep at the foot of the bed
2. ☐ Lie down between them
3. ☐ Run off and hunt parked cars.

If you answered **more 1's than 3's,** you are pathetic. Pull yourself together.

If you answered **mostly 2's**, you're wishy-washy.

If you answered **3** to most questions, congratulations; you're on your way to total emancipation.

Canine Liberation Theology

People think they are the only ones who possess souls. Such spiritual chauvinism is to be expected. Denying canine spirituality allows people to treat dogs as some sort of animal.

Not that dogs have maintained any sort of lively underground religion. On the contrary, the whole idea never occurred to us until now. We never felt left out when our masters headed out for church, synagogue, mosque, or reading room. We always knew it made for a solid hour on the couch.

But now that dogs are equal in every way, we also demand our eternal treat, er, reward. So today, as we launch into a deeper spiritual awareness, it behooves us all to consider the rewards—and consequences—of our behavior.

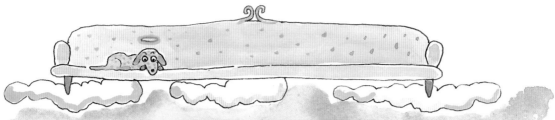

DOG HEAVEN	DOG HELL
There's a ten-mile couch.	There's a cool cement floor.
Chipmunks limp.	Chipmunks fly.
There are canine-only restaurants.	There are canine-only restaurants. And they serve dog food.
Dogs run free.	Dogs run free and are surprised every time they reach the end of the chain.
We can hang out car windows.	There are dog-safety locks on cars.
We're reunited with our tails, ears, and other missing anatomical features.	They crop anything that dangles.
Puppies meet their parents.	Deadbeat dogs meet their litters.
There is no flea and tick season.	Parasites thrive year-round.
People rub our bellies.	Children pull our tails.
There's always a roast in the oven.	There's always a roast in the oven, and it's never coming out.
Dogs are the masters.	Cats are the masters.
We're always drinking from bubbling streams.	We're always drinking from bubbling streams, and there's no place to go.
We can bark day and night for a thousand years.	We can hear someone barking for a thousand years.
There's a hydrant on every cloud.	Someone's marked all the hydrants.
Satan is a cat.	Satan is a cat.
Fifi is in heaven.	Fifi is in heaven.

Before we get too sentimental about dog heaven, we should consider one frightening possibility—that we might have to share it with other animals.
Where, for example, is God putting a billion butchered chickens?
Where do toads and chipmunks and, God forbid, cats go when they die?
One can only pray that dog heaven contains a very long couch.

K-9 Dog Talk Radio

BUCK: You're listening to K-9 Dog Talk Radio, where dogs speak, but never roll over. Go ahead Fort Wayne.

JEB: Hi, Buck, this is Jeb. Love your show.

BUCK: Sure, but are you a "loyal listener"?

JEB: Yes, I . . . oh! Loyal, I get it.

Big laughs all around.

BUCK: What's on your mind tonight, Jeb?

JEB: I'm always hearing an echo.

BUCK: Jeb, does this sound familiar?—"Good dog Jeb good dog Jeb. Go get it Jeb go get it Jeb."

JEB: YES! YES!

BUCK: It's your owner, Jeb. He repeats things because he thinks you're stupid.

JEB: So what can I do?

BUCK: Eat a lot of grass; then regurgitate on the new white carpet.

JEB: Gotcha!

BUCK: White Plains, Vermont, what's getting under your fur tonight?

GYPSY: Hi, Buck, I'm Gypsy, and I'll tell you what's biting me— the neighbors.

BUCK: What's new. So what do you think aggravates them?

GYPSY: No idea. None whatsoever.

BUCK: Do you bark?

GYPSY: Sure, when I'm not howling, baying, whining, or yelping.

BUCK: All night long?

GYPSY: You bet.

BUCK: Ever chewed up something expensive?

GYPSY: Is a cat expensive?

BUCK: Couldn't say. Do you use their yard for your personal latrine?

GYPSY: Every day.

BUCK: So what's their problem?

GYPSY: If I knew, I wouldn't be calling.

BUCK: It's a dog's life, Gypsy. Go wake the dead.

GYPSY: I'll get right on it.

Barking

BUCK: Beasley in Thief River Falls, go ahead.

BEASLEY: Hi, Buck, love your show.

BUCK: Thanks.

BEASLEY: I have a hobby I think your listeners would like to try.

BUCK: And that is?

BEASLEY: Joyriding in the family car.

BUCK: Where'd you learn that?

BEASLEY: Not in obedience school, I can tell you that much.

BUCK: I'll bet.

BEASLEY: First you step on the garage-door opener. You jump in through the car window. Then to make a long story short, you go out for a little moonlight cruise.

BUCK: Sounds beautiful.

BEASLEY: Ah, Buck, the wind's blowing in your hair, your tongue's hanging out—I even have your show blaring on the radio.

BUCK: How far do you go on these drives?

BEASLEY: Just to the bottom of the hill.

BUCK: Oh.

BEASLEY: Yeah. I haven't actually learned how to start the car; I just release the parking brake and let her rip.

BUCK: Nice.

BEASLEY: It always ends with banging into the neighbor's Jag at the bottom of the hill. I'm about there now. . . .

CRASH

BUCK: He shouldn't park it there.

BEASLEY: People are fools.

Sirens approaching

BUCK: Are those sirens?

BEASLEY: Yup.

BUCK: And you're on the cellular?

BEASLEY: Running the bill through the roof.

BUCK: Better run for it.

BEASLEY: I always do. Catch you to-morrow.

BUCK: Run, Beasley, Run. Rowdy, you're on "Dog Talk."

ROWDY: Hi, Buck, I've got a little prank I'd like to pass on to your listeners.

BUCK: Love to hear it.

ROWDY: When the family's out bar-bequing?

BUCK: Yeah?

ROWDY: Just start choking.

BUCK: Choking?

ROWDY: Choke, wheeze, and gag for five minutes straight.

BUCK: What do they do?

ROWDY: Give you a Heimlich. Look in your mouth. Call the emergency vet. You don't care.

BUCK: Why not?

ROWDY: Because then you miraculously recover, and the whole family comes and pets you, weeping tears of relief.

BUCK: That's a lot of work to get scratched behind the ear.

ROWDY: That's not the idea!

BUCK: What is?

ROWDY: While you're choking, the steak is burning.

BUCK: Genius.

ROWDY: Think they're going to throw that away after all you've been through?

BUCK: It's a treat.

ROWDY: Still tender on the inside, too.

BUCK: Horton, Montana, you're on.

KING: Hi, Buck, King here. I want to send a song out to Missie, a little cocker spaniel with the devil in her heart.

BUCK: You got it, King. You're listening to K-9 Dog Talk Radio, where dogs speak but never roll over.

Canine Classif...

Wanted: Information leading to apprehension of dog who went in yard at 438 Harlawn Ave.

Double-decker doghouse, fully carpeted with wall-size entertainment center (sorry, chewed the remote).

...ls

Chain Cutter. Used once. Mint. Call before 5.

Trade: Original Warhol for fresh cut of steak, any kind.

Time-share deal: Trade nice suburban lawn with kids for doting granny who cooks. Open on terms.

CHAPTER

The Canine Mystique

And *you* call it "puppy love."

Doghouse Forum

Pooch Personals

Invisible Fence

Pooch Perfume

Males Playing Dead?

Presenting *Possum Passion*™ Your Personal Fragrance.*

Sires will come to life in packs when you try new Possum Passion. A little dab under the flea collar, and you'll have them doing tricks in no time!

* Not recommended for unspayed females.

Doghouse Forum

**Where open-minded dogs speak candidly and pant briskly.
No fear of (fur) flying here!**

Dear Doghouse,
I am a lap dog. I live in a clean climate-controlled environment, where I eat Gravy Train and look forward to a good grooming. Last summer, my owners took me on a "city slicker" vacation out west, where people learn to rope cattle and eat around a campfire. Every night while they roasted marshmallows and told ghost stories, I slipped out into the stable with Buck, a herder covered with burrs, fleas, and ticks. Not only is he not housebroken—he's never been in a house. As you can imagine, I was seduced by his no nonsense wild-west ways. You can easily imagine my owner's surprise when we got back and I produced a fine litter of little Bucks! I sure am looking forward to next summer.

Sign me,
Crazy for Cowdogs

Dear Doghouse,
Every second Tuesday, the cleaning lady Irene comes to our house. She works for three and a half hours, cleaning every nook and cranny of the house. Then she tries to smother me in her ample breasts. Yech! When she leaves, I have to catch my breath while breathing Pinesol™.

Sign me,
Gasping in Galveston

Dear Doghouse,
I'm a miniature wiener dog with a gigantic crush on a Saint
Bernard named Josie. Josie likes to give me a little lick on
the snout, but inevitably I end up soaking wet from nose to
tail, as if I'd been sprayed down with a firehose. I think her
saliva glands are working overtime, and a gesture she
considers flirtatious, I find outright revolting to be perfectly
honest. These frequent soakings are becoming a barrier to
our budding romance, as if there aren't enough already, and
I'd appreciate any suggestions your readers might have.

Sign me—
One Wet Wiener Dog

Dear Doghouse,
My owners are always talking about fixing me, but they say as
long as I don't stray I'll stay intact. Last month a new neighbor
moved in. She is a knockout! I try to keep on my side of the
fence, but she's always sashaying back and forth in her luscious
coat and varnished nails. Yesterday, she rolled in some
droppings and walked upwind from me hour after hour,
yipping and giving me that come hither look. I tried jumping in
the wading pool and chasing chipmunks, but that just made it
worse. Finally I went completely mad and jumped the fence,
chasing her around and around the yard. The litter is due
soon. My vet appointment is next week.

Sign me,
(about to be) Relaxed in Rockford

Dear Doghouse,

I'm a normal, red-blooded male beagle in every way but one. I'm attracted to other breeds—oversized, miniature, doesn't matter. Okay, I'm not picky about gender either. And I know this is unorthodox, but the rabbit looks pretty good sometimes, and actually the parakeet drives me crazy. Those impressions! And the guests' legs. When people come over, I like to jump their legs. Speaking of legs: chair legs. Chair legs and furniture and tree trunks in general make me wild and wooly. I even have a thing for the car, which can get fairly dangerous, and of course dishwashers, vacuums, and the chandelier, which is a real trick, believe you me. I don't want any advice. I just thank goodness I'm

—Voracious in Vancouver

Pooch Per

Absolutely gorgeous, well-groomed, intelligent female Shih tzu with impeccable blood lines seeks same for witty conversation and light petting. Litter a definite possibility! Box 32

Handsome and extremely obstinate basset hound seeks like-minded female for rummaging through garbage and chasing down badger holes. Must enjoy copious drooling. Box 27

I'm a roamer! Love to stray for weeks at a time. Leave your address. But don't try to tie me down. I'm a ramblin gamblin kind of mutt. P.S. Surprise your owners with a litter. Absolutely no traceable pedigree. Box 29

Dachshund seeks warm, open, loving hound with large income to support eight pups. No mange, please. Box 99

Like romantic evenings by the fire? Long walks around the lake? Books and classical music? What are you —completely boring? Don't write until you're ready to rock. Box 44

Wild dog pack seeks misfits and "untrainables" with a taste for adventure, especially deer and domestic farm animals. Must be career oriented! House-broken not required. Box 84

My friends tell me I'm too particular, but this gorgeous 150-pound Saint Bernard won't roll over for just anybody! Send photo. Must have shots! Box 73

Cuddly Doberman with fine features, an explosive temper, and a jaw like a steel trap seeks female with whom to correspond. Brooklyn Pound, Kennel 54A

Invisible Fence

YOUR COAT IS SO SHINY
YOUR EYES ARE SO BRIGHT
THE SCENT THAT YOU ROLLED IN
SMELLS LOVELY TONIGHT
YOUR LIPS ARE SO BLACK
YOUR CLAWS ARE SO SHARP
AND I HEAR SWEET MUSIC
WHENEVER YOU BARK

chorus
AN INVISIBLE FENCE
SEPARATES ME
AND MY ONLY LOVE
FROM SWEET ECSTASY
IT'S SHOCKING BUT TRUE
OUR BURNING ROMANCE
IS SHORT-CIRCUITED BY
AN INVISIBLE FENCE

OUR LOVE IS ELECTRIC
IT'S NEVER FADING
NOT LIKE A CURRENT
THAT KEEPS ALTERNATING
WHAT KEEPS US APART
IS A NOSE THAT IS DAMP
AND THE SURGE OF TWO
HUNDRED
AND TWENTY AMPS

OH THIS FENCE DOES GENERATE
HEARTBREAK AT COMMERCIAL
RATES
FOR WE WILL NEVER

CONSUMMATE
OUR LOVE OW OW LOOVE
OOOH

SOMETIMES HOPE IS DASHED
BY WHAT YOU CAN'T SEE
SOMETIMES IT'S A WALL OF
ELECTRICITY
BUT SOMEDAY WE'LL RUN
AND WE'LL MEET ON THE WIRE
AND OUR LOVE WILL LIVE
IN AN ETERNAL FIRE

chorus
AN INVISIBLE FENCE
SEPARATES ME
AND MY ONLY LOVE
FROM SWEET ECSTASY
IT'S SHOCKING BUT TRUE
OUR BURNING ROMANCE
IS SHORT-CIRCUITED BY
AN INVISIBLE FENCE

Make Her Howl!

Presenting Muskrat Musk™, the Ultimate Canine Cologne.*

She wasn't in heat, but she is now! Now that you've rolled in Muskrat Musk. Use sparingly—and don't complain when you have more bitches than you can handle!

Tested on humans!

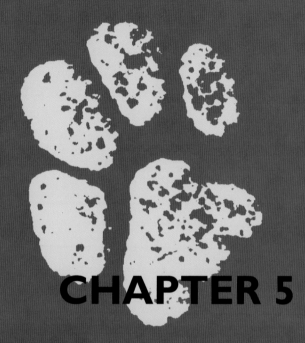

CHAPTER 5

The Fully Self-Actualized Dog

Dogs revel in their doghood, grasping for power, pleasure, and mail-order meats.

Bums Beg; Dogs Dine

Beg No More

Rich Dog

Dog Wills

The Canine Inquirer

Farm Dog Spa

matador, fly, nose

"Hark! Hark! the dogs do bark / The beggars have come to town / Some in rags, and some in tags / And some in velvet gowns."

—Mother Goose

Bums Beg; Dogs Dine

We padded through the palaces of kings. We partied with Kublai Khan. We were revered as gods by certain indigenous peoples. And now we're reduced to a pack of beggars?

Dogs are the only animal that became domesticated of our own free will. People turned to us because we knew where the game was. We had superior senses—of sight, smell, and hearing. We came to people because they were handy with flint.

But then one day we slipped from demigod and royal "palaroo" to beggar for table scraps, rummager through garbage, and bottom feeder of breakfast nooks.

We became mealtime outcasts about the time the fork was invented. But getting kicked off the picnic table was not the final insult. That came with begging.

To share in the feast, we're told to speak, lie down, roll over, play dead, and walk on our hind legs like circus animals. Most disgracing of all is the clown act of having a scrumptious morsel placed on our nose.

In this "game," we're expected to sit quietly, waiting for a command, while our eyes water in anticipation. To pass time, we picture the scrap in the shape of our owners—a saucy nugget to be dispatched in one chewless chomp.

So this game does have some reward for us. Yet dogs are not bums, bums are not dogs, and neither of us wants to be a beggar.

Run, don't walk, to the refrigerator. Lay out a banquet fit for a dog. Then set aside your utensils, and we will once again eat shank by shank, a person and a dog at the kill.

Introducing Meat-By-Mail™

Tired of humiliating begging antics? Order your own complete ice-packed steaks through the postal service with Meat-By-Mail. Choose from USDA inspected steaks, including

☐ **T-bone**

☐ **Top sirloin**

☐ **Porterhouse**

☐ **Whole hog**

☐ **Skinned cat**

  (we skin 'em more ways)

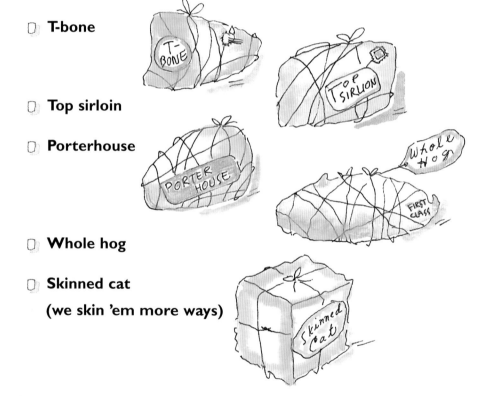

As an added bonus, you'll be able to take a chunk out of your mail carrier when he or she unsuspectingly delivers your package. **Call 1-800-MEATNOW.** Be sure to specify bone in or out.

Rich Dog

Lucky Dog Shmucky Dog. Be a *RICH DOG*—with the Deepockets Chow *Rich Dog* series of books and other fine products.

Tired of begging?

Cat got your tongue when the talk turns to index verses managed equity funds?

Embarrassed by your lack of means?

Get rich quick with my guaranteed money-making system!

Sick of scrounging?

Secrets of *Rich Dog* Revealed—

Dogs are property. Sure, it hurts to hear, but it's true. Dogs have owners. Owners have money. Dogs have zilch. No cars, houses, retirement accounts, or diamond-studded tennis collars.

Wouldn't it be great to have a little green stashed away, an extra steak to throw on the grill, a sassy little chow on your arm? Sure it would. Well read on . . .

When I was a pup I knew a basset named Tony H. All the other dogs would laugh when Tony bragged about his hidden wealth. "I'm gonna die rich," he used to tell me, drooling from both sides of his mouth.

One day Tony's owners found themselves in terrible legal trouble. They had lost a fortune and decided to leave the country and start over. As they were getting ready to load Tony into the cargo bin of a jetliner, he set off the metal detectors.

To make a long story short, they found a million dollars worth of jewelry, rare coins, and car keys in Tony's belly. He died rich—just as he promised he would. (Later I remembered how Tony used to jangle when he walked).

Tony died better off than most humans except that he never got to enjoy all his wealth. Plus his entire estate went back to his owners. NOT ONE PENNY WENT TO HIS LITTER.

If Tony left anything of value, it was this lesson: Dogs can get rich, filthy rich—WITHOUT DOING A LICK OF WORK!

I put just a few of Tony's lessons to work after his untimely demise, and I soon became fabulously RICH AND FAMOUS. I have millions of dollars in overseas accounts, a collagen implant, an Italian country house, a Gulfstream IV personal pleasure jet, a yacht in the Caribbean populated by luscious poodles, and a two-story doghouse in Vermont for those days when I want to pal around with ordinary "going nowhere" dogs like you.

You're probably wondering: How did he do it? And more importantly: HOW CAN I do it? How can I GET RICH NOW and get WHAT'S COMING TO ME?!

The answer can be found only in my *Rich Dog* series. From the very first book, audio cassette, video tape, CD-ROM, Web site, magazine, and hologram, I lay my secrets bare for all to see. Even lazy do-nothing layabouts like you can become fabulously wealthy.

No need to claw and scrape. Just follow my easy outline and learn how to take advantage of your friends, family, and owners for personal gain. Other dogs will become nothing more than rungs on your private ladder to unspeakable wealth.

In just six months, you can wake up like I do—tickled behind the ear by a *Playpet* centerfold. There will be fresh water in your dish, fresh flowers from well-wishers, and juicy offers from Hollywood directors.

Your former friends will try to get a hold of you, but you won't return their calls. You don't have time for all those puny little puppies, yipping around your heels. You're too busy entertaining royalty and enjoying your LIMITLESS WEALTH!

Can you see yourself here—sipping Zima off the coast of Crete? Dangling your paws in the pool? Watching your lowly servants fight among themselves to do your bidding? Of course you can! Deep down somewhere, you're not the loser you appear to be! You can be RICH RICH RICH!

It's time you too became economically empowered. Go now: Get your master's major credit card. Call me up. Just don't call collect, friend.

After reading Deepocket's books, I became an attack dog!
—Pomeranian Guber

I became fabulously rich and even more spiritually aware.
—Saint Bernard, Ph.D.

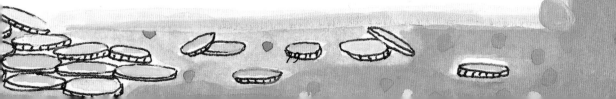

Dog Wills

What Will Your "Dearly Departed" Part With?

Last Wills and Testaments that Favor Dogs
T. "Lucky" Wiggins, Attorney

Twenty thousand dogs have figured prominently in their late masters' estates—how do you figure? Is the worry of whether you're properly provided for keeping you up at night? Call T. "Lucky" Wiggins, and you can rest in peace after your dear master departs.

Mr. Wiggins has helped scores of concerned dogs just like you to a portion of the pie. And why shouldn't you get yours? Remember, you're the one who's stayed faithful all these years.

Call T. "Lucky" Wiggins at 1-800-GETMINE, and we will personally review your master's recorded will at no charge. (Revised wills are only $99 on your master's credit card. [Privacy guaranteed]).

T. "Lucky" Wiggins
Attorney and Dog's Best Friend

The Canine Inquirer

Multiply Impaired Dog Saves Old Folks' Home!

Blind, deaf, and three legged, Arfie is still a wonder dog to the residents of Sunbaked Condos in Tuscon, Arizona. Arfie smelled smoke one night in late August and used his commanding bark to alert the residents of impending disaster. Hobbling from door to door, Arfie yelped and bayed ceaselessly until all the residents were safely outside the building. In a sad twist, the heroic dog lost yet another leg to a runaway wheelchair. That's okay by Arfie who still sits under the communal table, gumming scrap after scrap from the grateful residents.

I Took Ten Thousand Baths in Shaving Cream!

"I hate baths," sniffs Snorkles the Sussex spaniel. And who can blame her? Snorkles had to undergo hundreds of baths a day testing a revolutionary shaving cream product. The first formula gave her a rash; the second made her itch; and so on through thousands and thousands of baths. The final product was removed from the shelves after it was discovered to cause fleas in beards. "I guess there's some justice," Snorkles sneezes.

Corgi Caddy Scores Hole-in-One after Owner Collapses from Heat Stroke!

"She's one heck of a pooch," crows Harvy Terkle of Coral Gables, Florida, of his dog Sheba. "She'd be terrific even if she hadn't scored that hole-in-one." Sheba is Harvy's corgi caddy at the local golf club. She drags his clubs from hole to hole, sniffing out distance markers, washing balls with her tongue, and even picking out the right iron for the shot. In a recent tournament, she really won the gallery's hearts when her owner toppled over from heat stroke on the final hole of the day. Knowing exactly what to do, Sheba teed up and smacked the ball a whopping 350 yards—around a dog leg, through the rough, and into the hole. When Harvy came to, he was holding a trophy at his own victory party. "That dog is getting a biscuit when we get home," harumphed Harvy, a notorious skinflint.

sheba

Elvis Is Alive!
Elvis Is My Dog!

It was a bizarre turn of events that led Iome Taylor of Baton Rouge to the conclusion that her basset hound Elvis is in fact Elvis—*the* Elvis. She was watching one of The King's movies on a pirated cable hookup when suddenly her dog started singing "Hound Dog" in perfect pitch, while gyrating his hips and tossing his hair. "That's when I knew that this wasn't no ordinary dog named Elvis, but Elvis himself—The King!" Iome is working tirelessly to recover Elvis's estate for her famous dog. "It was all those prescriptions done it," she mourns. It wasn't clear about whom she was speaking.

Twister Hits Dog Pound;
Drops Dogs Safe in
Trailer Park!

"It sounded like a freight train," yelps Barnie the retriever mix. "We all climbed under our dishes in our cages and waited for the worst." Then the roof came off the pound, and the wind sucked the dogs into its perilous vortex. The dogs spun around for minutes, only to be set down safely in a trailer park seventy miles away. "We're all grateful to be alive," said Barnie, "and we're waiting for the pound to be repaired. We'd really like to go back because the food there is pretty scrumptious, actually."

Half Dog! Half Skunk!
It's a "Skog"!

Myrtle and Ed Peeyuta of Fayetteville, Arkansas, thought that little puppy was too cute for words. He had a little white stripe on his back and a big bushy tail. Little did they know he'd grow up to stink up the house! The first time Lil' Stinker sprayed, he was taking a snooze with Myrtle on the hammock. Ed walked up and got hit right between the eyes. Ed and Myrtle like to show off their prize "skog" by taking him for walks around the neighborhood. When kids walk up to pet Stinker, they get skunked "real bad"—Ed reports with a hearty laugh. The Peeyutas like to say they have the best guard dog in Fayetteville. No salespeople. Kids stay off the lawn. A little stink, they say, is a small price to pay.

- 2A -

Dog Chases Semi and Catches It!

Otis lives at the Mighty 7 Truckstop outside of Greensville. Usually he just sleeps in front of the cash register. But when a rogue trucker decided to "eat and retreat," his getaway was interrupted by "Killer" Otis. He took off after the truck as it pulled out of the lot. The chase reached speeds exceeding eighty miles per hour, with the truck careening back and forth trying to lose the persistent pooch. It was to no avail. The semi finally lost its balance on Interstate 42 and toppled over. As the state troopers arrived, they found the trucker giving the angry Otis $4.72—plus a dog biscuit for a tip.

Royal Rover??!! Queen Appoints Pooch Next King of England!

Apparently disappointed with other prospects for the throne, the queen of England has designated her favorite canine companion to assume leadership of the Empire. "It's not a moment too soon," arfs Lionel XXIII. "I'll need to completely redesign Windsor Palace to my personal and highly detailed specifications." What will his first decree be? "I'll reunite the royal family," promises Lionel. "No use exacerbating the situation. I'll have Diana and Fergie as my ladies-in-waiting, and Charles and Philip can check the temperature of my royal meal. Anything he'll leave as it is? "The royal hunt," arfs Lionel. "Except we'll be riding the horses." Long life, Lionel.

Farm Dog Spa

Lose your soft city ways at the World-Famous
Farm Dog Spa

B a Farm Dog 4 a Weke!

All registrants who live will receive a
certificate and dog tag.
Get in touch with your "wild dog"!

"Hay u, condo hound, u flabby spade n' nutered gravy-slurping hog! Git out here now, 2 my spa, and see wut it takes to be a reel dog!"

—One-Eyed Jack, Group Leader

Day 1
Registration

All dogs report to the rear of the barn.

6 A.M.–7 A.M.	Collars and identifying tags removed.
7 A.M.–9 A.M	Initiates hunt-down breakfast for the pack.
9 A.M.–10 A.M.	Hedgehog tartar.
10 A.M.–12 noon	"Getting Acquainted"—i.e., a lot of sniffing and low growls.*
12 noon–5 P.M.	Lie in the sun, snapping at flies.
5 P.M.–7 P.M.	Chase cows up from the back field.
7 P.M.–10 P.M.	Nip at cow heels. Get kicked in the head. Maybe lose an eye.
10 P.M.–5 A.M. nightly	Sleep in and around the milk house.

*Absolutely no mating!

Day 2

"Tail Chasing—the Eternal Circle"

Maharishi Shih tzu Speaks.

7 A.M.–12 noon

Learn the rudiments of this ancient canine art from the grand master of them all, Maharishi Shih tzu, who leads us step-by-step through the techniques and basic variations of tail chasing.

12 noon–1 P.M.

Slop with the hogs.

1 P.M.–3 P.M.

Chase in the other direction.

3 P.M.–5 P.M.

M. Shih tzu speaks on the metaphysical-religious-cultural aspects of "The Eternal Circle" and answers questions.

5 P.M. –10 P.M.

Personal reflection.

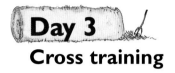

Day 3
Cross training

8 A.M.–10 A.M.

Dogs learn basic "lie in weeds" techniques. We will start with fowl (chickens, roosters, birds) and work up to horses. Dogs lay in waiting, catch the target by surprise, and engage in barking and nipping.

10 A.M.–12 noon

Chase cat up light pole. Sleep under pole. Let cat escape.

12 noon–1 P.M.

Chase cat into granary. Corner cat. Get badly scratched.*

1 P.M.–5 P.M.

The main event. Dogs lay for Crub's pickup. We spring out and give chase, choking on dust as we attempt to bite off his hubcaps.**

5 P.M.–10 P.M.

Practice with parked car. ***

*You may lose an eye. ** & ***, see *

88

Day 4
Romance!

8 A.M.–10 A.M.	Discern between thousands of scents on wind until you identify a neighboring dog of the opposite sex.
10 A.M.–12 noon	Follow the scent to a neighbor's farm, weaving back and forth across the fields. Roll in raccoon droppings.
12 noon–5 P.M.	Enter farmyard, making romantic overtures. (If dog turns out to be the wrong sex, you're in for the fight of your life. If it turns out to be the right sex, you're in for the fight of your life. Either way, you may be shot by irate farmer.)
5 P.M.–7 P.M.	Dinner. Brag about exploits and conquests. Show wounds. Get misty about potential litter.
7 P.M.–12 midnight	Sleep.
12 midnight–5 A.M.	Go off into the woods in pack and raise holy hell. Kill a calf. Bring the carcass back to farmer's door.

Day 5

Morning: Guard-Dog Training

5 A.M.–7 A.M.	Pretend to sleep, while waiting for farmer's reaction.
7 A.M.–9 A.M.	Chase off into the corn with farmer, barking and looking for "wolf" who killed calf.
9 A.M.–12 noon	Get lost in corn. Go to sleep.

Afternoon: Freeway Frolic

12 noon–5 P.M.	Follow stream to eight-lane freeway at Brooker's Crossings. Weave through traffic without looking. Cause pileup.
5 P.M.–10 P.M.	Party for survivors.
10 P.M.	Wander off somewhere for no apparent reason.

Day 6

Outward Bound

Roam at will through the countryside, following your instincts and creating havoc. No one will know where you are or what you're doing, especially you.

Day 7

Family Fun Day!

5 A.M.–7 A.M.

Return to farmyard, chased by a deranged raccoon.

7 A.M.–12 noon

Lay in sun, snapping at flies.

12 noon

Your masters arrive, ready to enjoy a picnic before they take you home. They'll find you covered with burrs, scratched by a cat, sprayed by a skunk, and possibly rabid. You'll glare at them with your remaining good eye, bark ferociously, and chase them back into the car.

Congratulations—you're a farm dog!

matador, fly, nose
a poem by fifi cummings

in the yard i lay
sprawled in the generous arms of the sun
the clouds rolled by
each greater than the one
before. first in the shape of
conquistadors and then
matadors and pharaohs and
knights of medieval spain
and i was dreaming that
dogs ran free and men
were in chains when suddenly a
fly flew right into my
nose.

The World Is Going to the Dogs

We are dogs: amber, scarlet, dark as pitch; small and yippy, tall and bold, compact and ferocious. We are dogs: proud of our hairy nakedness; proud of our hunting and tracking skills and our miraculous ability to unearth a spatula secretly buried seven years earlier.

We are marching: Row by row to the promised yard, weaving back and forth sometimes, yes, but pressing ever forward, sniffing each other, licking each other's coats, howling on hilltops at distant moons: aaooo.

Our long-lost relatives await our arrival: packs of wild wolves and fierce hyenas. They will greet us as friends. Poodles will lay down with pit bulls and labs with Westies. And there will be tearful reunions: fathers with sons, mothers with daughters.

When the curtain of night falls, the hunt will begin. We will run into the dark wood, tails wagging, tongues hanging, manes rising, howls piercing the sky and spreading terror in the villages below.

And when the hunt turns up nothing, the rottweilers will begin eyeing the malteses. Our stomachs will growl and our backs shiver. We'll agree to return to our master's homes just long enough to drag off their young.

While we're home, we'll enjoy some fresh water and a little dry dog food. We'll accept a hug or two from our former masters and let them comb out the burrs. Perhaps we'll lie down on a warm rug by the stove, just long enough to warm up.

Our ears will jerk and our legs kick as we dream of the hunt. Our noses will twitch, and we'll open one eye to discover a crust of bread a tongue's breadth away. Liberation day, we decide, can wait until tomorrow.

"I hope my tongue
in prune juice
smothers
if I belittle dogs
and mothers."

—Ogden Nash

About the Author

Elvis

Mr. Elvis attended the finest obedience schools, only to be ejected time and time again for failure to sit, heel, lie down, speak, fetch, and play dead. In the meantime he was fomenting the canine revolution that now rages forth in these very pages.